Course Creator's Gold

Build Interactive Courses that Stick and SELL!

Meek Dual

Copyright © 2024 Meek Dual

All rights reserved.

ISBN: 9798343961270

DEDICATION

To and for Pookie.

CONTENTS

PREFACE: *Why I Wrote This Book* 1

   How to Get the Most Value from This Book....................2

INTRODUCTION: *The Power of Engaging Courses* 4

CHAPTER 1: *The Gold Standard: What Makes a Course High-Value* 7

   High-Perceived Value: More Than Just Content.............8

   Why Perceived Value Matters in a Crowded Market 8

   The Key Elements of High-Value Courses 9

   Real-World Examples of High-Value Courses 10

CHAPTER 2: *Understanding Your Audience: Designing for Engagement* 13

   Why Audience Understanding is Essential for Engagement..14

   Creating Detailed Audience Avatars for Your Course...14

   Identifying Pain Points and Learning Goals to Shape Content..16

   Building Content That Resonates Emotionally and Intellectually 17

Gathering Feedback and Insights Before Creating Your Course 18

CHAPTER 3: *Crafting Course Goals That Inspire* 21

The Power of Specific, Inspiring Course Goals 22

Defining Clear, Achievable, and Motivating Course Goals 22

Aligning Goals with Audience Needs 24

Crafting Goals that Promise Transformation 25

Keeping Learners Motivated with a Clear Learning Path 26

CHAPTER 4: *Building Interactive and Dynamic Learning* .. 29

Why Engagement Requires Thoughtful Interaction 29

Tools and Strategies for Creating Interaction 30

Incorporating Storytelling and Scenarios to Deepen Engagement 33

Using Gamification to Make Learning Fun and Sticky .. 34

CHAPTER 5: *Enhancing Perceived Value with Visual and Emotional Design* 37

Design Matters: How Presentation Influences Perceived Value 38

Best Practices for Designing a Visually Appealing Course Interface 38

Building Emotional Resonance Through Design 40

Creating a Cohesive, Professional Aesthetic that Boosts Credibility 41

CHAPTER 6: *Positioning and Marketing Your High-Value Course* 44

The Power of Positioning: How Marketing Impacts Perceived Value 45

Identifying Your Unique Selling Proposition (USP) 45

Crafting Irresistible Course Descriptions That Focus on Transformation 46

Leveraging Testimonials and Social Proof to Build Trust 48

Positioning Your Course as the Must-Have Solution 49

Crafting Sales Copy That Converts 50

CHAPTER 7: *Pricing for Profit and Value* 53

Pricing Communicates Value: Why Pricing Matters 54

The Psychology of Pricing: Why Charging More Can Increase Perceived Value 54

Balancing Affordability and Profitability 56

Offering Tiered Pricing or Premium Packages 57

Maximizing Profit While Maintaining High Perceived Value 59

CHAPTER 8: *Building a Supportive Community* 61

Why Community Matters: Enhancing Learning and Increasing Value 62

How to Build and Manage a Thriving Community 62

Tools and Platforms for Building an Engaging Learning Community 65

Practical Tips for Building a Learning Community That Lasts 66

CHAPTER 9: *Ongoing Support and Course Optimization* .. 69

Why Continuous Support and Optimization Matter 69

Offering Ongoing Support: Keeping Learners Engaged Beyond the Course 70

Using Feedback and Data to Improve Future Versions of Your Course 72

Creating Alumni Groups and Offering Long-Term Engagement 73

CHAPTER 10: *Scaling Your Course Business* 76

From Single Course to Course Empire: The Power of Scaling...76

Leveraging Automation to Free Up Your Time.............77

Expanding Your Offerings: Bundles, Masterclasses, and Certifications...78

Partnering with Influencers and Experts to Expand Your Reach..80

Turning a One-Time Course Into an Evergreen Revenue Stream..81

CONCLUSION: *Your Gold Standard for Course Creation*...84

Your Time to Shine: Step Into Your Power as a Course Creator...85

BOOKS IN THIS SERIES: *The Course Creator's Toolkit*.......87

Book 1: The Authority Advantage: Build Your Influence, Impact, and Income by Sharing What You Know..........88

Book 2: Course Creator's Gold: Build Interactive Courses that Stick and SELL..89

Book 3: Followers to Friends: Build Authentic Connections and Lasting Success Online.......................91

ABOUT THE AUTHOR...93

ACKNOWLEDGMENTS

First and foremost, I want to thank my amazing son, **Tyler Jackson**. Tyler, you've been my rock, my constant support, and my greatest motivation. Thank you for stepping up at home, making sure I had the space and time to write, and always cheering me on with that infectious enthusiasm. I couldn't have done this without you.

To my best friend and right-hand, **Feliciann Malloy**, thank you for being my partner in both work and life. You've kept me grounded and focused, especially when things got tough. Your support has been unwavering, and I'm beyond grateful for all the ways you've helped me build this business. You've been there through every challenge, every late-night brainstorm, and every triumph.

Lastly, a heartfelt thank you to my incredible clients. You've trusted me, been patient, and allowed me the space to grow and refine my system. Your belief in me has meant the world, and I'm honored to be a part of your journey as you build your own success.

This book is a reflection of all the love, support, and dedication from the people around me. I am deeply grateful to each and every one of you.

.

PREFACE:
Why I Wrote This Book

I've spent years working with entrepreneurs, professionals, and creators who have an incredible amount of expertise to share with the world. But time and time again, I've seen these talented individuals struggle to turn their knowledge into engaging, high-value courses that sell. Many of them feel overwhelmed by the process—unsure of how to create a course that's not only informative but also captivating enough to stand out in today's crowded online marketplace.

That's why I wrote **"Course Creator's Gold: Build Interactive Courses that Stick and SELL."** My goal is to give you a clear, actionable roadmap to transform your expertise into a profitable course that not only educates but inspires your learners. I want to show you that creating a high-value course doesn't have to be complicated or intimidating—you just need the right strategy.

This book is about more than just making money from online courses. It's about empowering women like you to step into your role as experts, to share your brilliance with the world, and to build something that leaves a lasting impact. Whether you're just starting out or looking to scale an existing course, this book is designed to guide you through every step of the journey.

How to Get the Most Value from This Book

To help you make the most of the strategies in this book, I've created a companion workbook that you can download for free. The **"Course Creator's Gold Workbook"** will guide you through exercises, worksheets, and practical steps for each chapter, helping you put the principles into action and build a course that's uniquely yours.

You can download the FREE workbook at meekdual.com/coursegold.

Here's how you can maximize the value of this book:

1. **Follow the Steps in Order**: Each chapter builds on the last, taking you from idea to implementation. I recommend reading through the book in sequence to fully grasp the strategies and best practices.

2. **Complete the Workbook**: As you work through the book, use the workbook to apply the concepts to your own course. The exercises will help you clarify your course goals, design interactive experiences, and create a marketing strategy that sets your course up for success.

3. **Take Action**: The insights in this book are only as valuable as the actions you take. As you move through each chapter, start applying the strategies right away. You don't have to wait until you finish

the entire book—implement what resonates with you as you go.

4. **Build Your Community**: Engaging with others on the same journey is a great way to stay motivated and inspired. Whether you're building a community around your course or connecting with other course creators, don't go it alone.

By the time you finish this book, you'll have a clear plan for creating a high-value, engaging course that will not only sell but also create real transformation for your students. I'm excited for you to take the next step in your journey as a course creator and turn your expertise into gold.

Let's get started.

— Meek Dual

INTRODUCTION:
The Power of Engaging Courses

When Maya first launched her online course, she thought she had everything figured out. As an expert in wellness coaching, she poured her heart into creating content that was informative and backed by years of experience. But after months of effort, her course barely made a ripple in the market. The few students who signed up struggled to stay engaged, and despite her expertise, Maya found herself wondering what went wrong. Her content was valuable—so why wasn't it resonating? It wasn't until she focused on engagement and perceived value that everything changed. By adding interactive elements, fostering a supportive community, and making the learning experience truly memorable, Maya transformed her course from a lackluster offering into a thriving success, packed with loyal students eager to recommend her program to others.

If you're reading this, you've probably experienced similar frustrations. You've worked hard to create your course—you know your material inside and out—but it just doesn't seem to land with your audience. Maybe you feel overwhelmed by the process of course design or your content feels flat, not engaging students in the way you hoped. Worse, you may be struggling to convert learners into loyal customers or struggling to differentiate your course in a saturated market.

Creating an engaging course isn't just about cramming it full of information. It's about delivering an experience that not only educates but also captivates. Learners today have higher expectations than ever before. They want to be inspired, engaged, and feel like they are part of something bigger than a simple video lesson. Courses that can achieve this stand out, and they *sell*.

That's where this book comes in. **"Course Creator's Gold: Build Interactive Courses that Stick and Sell"** is your roadmap to designing high-value courses that engage your audience, create lasting impact, and drive profit. You'll learn how to build interactive learning experiences that resonate with your students, keep them excited, and make your content truly stick. Whether you're an experienced educator or just starting to explore course creation, this book will show you how to take your expertise and turn it into a captivating course that learners will love—and one that brings in real revenue.

I've been where you are. When I first ventured into course creation, I struggled with many of the same challenges you may be facing right now. I knew I had valuable knowledge to share, but I felt lost when it came to translating that expertise into an engaging learning experience. Like many first-time course creators, I focused on delivering information rather than designing an experience. It wasn't until I began integrating storytelling, interactivity, and real-world applications that everything clicked. My courses not only became more engaging, but they also became more profitable. The transformation in my business was dramatic, and I've since helped countless women do the same—create courses that stand out, inspire, and sell.

Now, I'm here to help you do the same. This book will guide you through the entire process of creating courses that stick—courses that not only impart knowledge but also keep learners engaged and eager for more. Together, we'll explore proven strategies for crafting high-perceived value, interactive learning experiences that turn students into lifelong customers.

By the end of this journey, you'll have all the tools you need to create a course that not only changes your students' lives but also grows your business. So, are you ready to take the next step? Let's dive in and turn your expertise into **gold**.

.

CHAPTER 1:
The Gold Standard: What Makes a Course High-Value

When my coworker Emily launched her first course on personal finance, she believed that her deep knowledge of the subject would be enough to attract students. She filled her modules with detailed lessons on budgeting, saving, and investing. But despite the valuable content, the course failed to gain traction. Students signed up but dropped off midway through, and few left positive reviews. Frustrated, Emily decided to pivot. She revamped her course, focusing on how the *experience* made students feel. She created a visually stunning design, incorporated interactive exercises, and built a strong community around the course. Almost overnight, her course transformed. Not only did more students enroll, but they also stayed engaged, shared rave reviews, and recommended the course to others. By focusing on *perceived value*, Emily didn't just sell a course—she created an experience that resonated with her learners.

High-Perceived Value: More Than Just Content

Emily's story illustrates a critical lesson for course creators: a high-perceived value course is about *more than just content*. You may be an expert in your field, but in today's crowded online market, learners aren't just looking for information—they're looking for memorable, engaging, and transformative experiences.

So, what is *perceived value*, and why does it matter so much? In a world where hundreds, if not thousands, of courses are available on any given subject, your course must stand out. And while having excellent content is important, it's not enough on its own. Perceived value is the overall impression your course gives students—how it looks, feels, and delivers its promise. When a course feels high in value, students are more likely to trust the instructor, stay engaged, and view the course as worth their investment of both time and money.

A high-value course isn't just one that delivers facts; it's one that creates a lasting impact on students, keeps them engaged from start to finish, and leaves them feeling transformed.

Why Perceived Value Matters in a Crowded Market

In the booming world of online education, learners are spoiled for choice. For every topic, there are endless options available, many at various price points. This means that as a course creator, you must go beyond simply offering *knowledge*. You have to create something that feels *different*—something that makes potential students feel like they are investing in an experience that is worth their time, energy, and money.

Perceived value is what sets apart a $20 course from a $200 or $2,000 course, even if the underlying content is similar. It's the reason why some courses, regardless of the topic, consistently attract students who are willing to pay a premium. Learners want to feel that they are getting more than just lessons—they want an experience that delivers transformation, connection, and impact.

The Key Elements of High-Value Courses

So, how do you design a course that conveys high value? Let's break down the essential elements:

1. **Presentation** The way your course *looks* and *feels* is one of the first things potential students will notice. A professional, visually appealing design creates an immediate sense of trust and credibility. This includes everything from the course platform and interface to the branding and aesthetic. Does your course look polished and well-organized? Is the layout intuitive and easy to navigate? A clean, professional presentation signals to learners that your course is worth their investment.

2. **Engagement** High-perceived value courses don't just lecture to students—they *engage* them. Learners should be actively involved in the process through interactive elements like quizzes, discussion forums, live Q&A sessions, or group projects. Engaging courses encourage participation and keep learners motivated, which makes the experience feel more valuable. Remember, it's not about how much content you can push at your students—it's about

how deeply you can involve them in their own learning journey.

3. **Actionable Outcomes** A high-value course should leave learners with more than just knowledge; it should provide *actionable outcomes* that they can immediately apply to their lives or careers. Your students should feel like they've walked away with something tangible—whether it's a new skill, a framework for solving problems, or a roadmap for personal growth. The more actionable and practical your content is, the higher the perceived value of the course.

4. **Support Systems** One of the most overlooked elements of a high-value course is the support system that surrounds it. Learners are more likely to stay engaged and complete the course if they feel supported. This can take the form of responsive instructor feedback, mentorship opportunities, community interaction, or even regular check-ins. Building a supportive environment shows learners that you care about their success, which significantly increases perceived value.

Real-World Examples of High-Value Courses

Let's take a look at two women who have mastered the art of creating high-perceived value in their courses:

- **Marie's Wellness Program**: Marie, a wellness coach, used to struggle with getting her course to stand out. She realized that while her content was valuable, it didn't *feel* different from other wellness courses in the market. After investing in high-quality video production, adding a community element where learners could connect and share their journeys, and creating personalized action plans for her students, she was able to elevate her course's perceived value. The result? Higher enrollment, rave reviews, and returning students eager for her next offering.

- **Jenna's Photography Course**: Jenna, a professional photographer, transformed her beginner's photography course by focusing on engagement. Rather than just delivering modules on techniques, she integrated interactive critiques, live photo challenges, and opportunities for students to showcase their work. By turning her course into a hands-on learning experience, Jenna created an immersive environment that kept her students engaged and eager for more. Her course quickly became one of the most popular in her niche, despite the crowded market.

Key Takeaways

By now, you understand that a high-value course is about *more* than just the content. Here are the core principles to keep in mind as you design your own high-perceived value course:

1. **Presentation Matters**: Ensure that your course looks professional, polished, and easy to navigate.

First impressions count, and a sleek design signals that your course is worth the investment.

2. **Engagement is Key**: Use interactive elements to keep your learners involved. Engagement doesn't just improve learning outcomes—it also boosts perceived value.

3. **Actionable Outcomes**: Make sure your students walk away with tangible, actionable insights. High-value courses offer more than knowledge—they provide clear, applicable results.

4. **Support Systems Boost Value**: Offer personalized feedback, mentorship, and community engagement to create a supportive learning environment that fosters student success.

By focusing on these elements, you can build a course that not only stands out in a crowded market but also creates lasting transformation for your students. And as your course's perceived value rises, so will your sales.

In the next chapter, we'll dive deeper into understanding your audience—because creating a high-value course starts with knowing exactly who you're designing for and what they need.

CHAPTER 2:
Understanding Your Audience: Designing for Engagement

When Sarah launched her first online course on digital marketing, she believed that covering every topic under the sun would make her course appealing to a broad audience. She filled the modules with hours of content on SEO, social media strategies, email marketing, and more. But despite her best efforts, her students weren't engaging. Many stopped halfway through the course, and her completion rates were abysmal. Determined to turn things around, Sarah took a step back and started listening to her audience. Through surveys and direct feedback, she learned that her students, mostly small business owners, were overwhelmed by too much information and needed practical, step-by-step solutions rather than an information overload. By realigning her course to focus specifically on content marketing strategies for small businesses—something her audience truly needed—Sarah saw an immediate transformation. Engagement skyrocketed, completion rates soared, and her students couldn't stop raving about how relevant and helpful her course had become.

Why Audience Understanding is Essential for Engagement

Sarah's story underscores a crucial truth in course creation: your content is only as good as its relevance to your audience. You can create the most polished, information-packed course, but if it doesn't meet the specific needs of your learners, it will fail to engage them. Understanding your audience deeply is the foundation of designing a course that not only grabs their attention but holds it, leading them to take action, complete the course, and recommend it to others.

Knowing who your audience is—what they struggle with, what their goals are, and how they learn best—is the key to creating a high-value course that resonates both emotionally and intellectually. When your content aligns with your learners' needs, you create an experience that feels personal, relevant, and transformative.

Creating Detailed Audience Avatars for Your Course

To design a course that truly engages, you must start by getting crystal clear on who your audience is. The best way to do this is by creating **audience avatars**—detailed profiles of your ideal learners. These avatars help you visualize your audience's characteristics, pain points, goals, and motivations, which allows you to tailor your content to meet their needs.

Here's how to create a detailed audience avatar:

1. **Demographics**: Start by outlining basic demographic information. What is the average age, gender, and education level of your target audience? Are they professionals, stay-at-home parents, or recent graduates? Understanding these basics will help you tailor your language, examples, and even the structure of your course.

2. **Psychographics**: Dive deeper by exploring the values, interests, and behaviors of your audience. What are their aspirations? Do they value time efficiency? Are they motivated by personal development or professional growth? These insights help you tap into what emotionally drives your audience.

3. **Pain Points**: What challenges and frustrations are your audience facing? For Sarah's audience, the pain point was the overwhelming amount of marketing information they were trying to manage. Identifying these pain points allows you to address them head-on in your course, creating a solution-based learning experience that feels tailored to your students' struggles.

4. **Learning Goals**: What specific outcomes does your audience want to achieve? Are they looking for a new skill? A career boost? Or maybe they want to solve a specific problem in their personal or professional life. Understanding these goals will help you shape your course content so that it delivers exactly what your students are looking for.

By creating detailed audience avatars, you'll have a clearer picture of who you are speaking to in your course, making it easier to craft content that truly resonates.

Identifying Pain Points and Learning Goals to Shape Content

Once you've built your audience avatar, the next step is to dive deeper into their pain points and learning goals. Understanding *what* your audience is struggling with and *where* they want to go is critical for shaping content that feels purposeful and relevant.

Here's how to do it:

1. **Ask the Right Questions**: Survey your potential students or engage in conversations with your existing audience. What challenges are they facing in relation to the course topic? What's preventing them from achieving their goals? What gaps do they feel in their current knowledge or skills?

2. **Analyze Common Struggles**: Look for patterns in the feedback you receive. Are there recurring frustrations or challenges that multiple people mention? These are the areas where your course can deliver the most value.

3. **Set Clear Outcomes**: Based on your audience's pain points, outline specific outcomes that your course will deliver. For example, if your audience struggles with time management in running a business, your course might promise to teach them how to automate key processes or create efficient workflows. When your course outcomes directly

address your audience's needs, they are more likely to stay engaged and complete the program.

By aligning your course content with the pain points and learning goals of your audience, you create a learning experience that feels highly relevant, which significantly boosts engagement.

Building Content That Resonates Emotionally and Intellectually

Creating content that resonates with your audience is about striking the right balance between emotional and intellectual engagement.

1. **Emotional Resonance**: When learners feel that you *understand* them—when your content speaks to their struggles, fears, and aspirations—they are more likely to connect with and trust you. Sharing stories, examples, or case studies that reflect their journey makes your course feel personal. For instance, sharing your own struggles (or those of others) with the topic at hand helps build a bridge between you and your students, showing them that you've been where they are and you know the path forward.

2. **Intellectual Engagement**: On the intellectual side, your content needs to challenge your audience, but in a way that feels achievable. Provide actionable, step-by-step instructions, practical strategies, and real-world applications that they can implement immediately. When learners feel they are gaining insights they can use right away, it reinforces their commitment to the course.

An emotionally resonant course fosters connection, while an intellectually engaging course builds credibility. Together, these two elements create a powerful learning experience that keeps students invested.

Gathering Feedback and Insights Before Creating Your Course

Before you even begin building your course, it's essential to gather feedback and insights from your potential audience. This ensures that you're creating a course that directly addresses their needs and helps you avoid the mistake of designing content based on assumptions.

Here are some actionable steps to gather valuable feedback:

1. **Conduct Surveys**: Send out surveys to your email list or social media followers asking specific questions about their biggest challenges related to your course topic. For example, "What's your biggest struggle when it comes to [your course subject]?" The answers will guide the structure and focus of your course.

2. **Engage in Conversations**: Join online communities or groups where your target audience hangs out. Pay attention to the discussions happening around your course topic. What are people asking? What frustrations are they expressing? Directly engaging with potential students can give you insights into their most pressing needs.

3. **Test Your Ideas**: Before fully committing to a course, try offering a smaller, beta version of your

program to a select group. This allows you to test your content, gather feedback, and make adjustments before launching the full course. It's an effective way to ensure that your course content is aligned with your audience's expectations.

4. **Create Polls or Q&A Sessions**: Use social media polls or host Q&A sessions to ask quick, targeted questions about your course idea. For example, "Would you prefer a course focused on [Topic A] or [Topic B]?" Engaging your audience in this way helps them feel involved in the creation process and gives you a clearer direction for your course.

By taking the time to gather insights and feedback, you ensure that the course you create is one that people *want* and *need*, rather than something you think they need.

Key Takeaways

Understanding your audience is the cornerstone of creating a course that truly engages. When you take the time to deeply understand who your learners are, what they struggle with, and what they want to achieve, you position yourself to create a course that resonates on both an emotional and intellectual level.

1. **Know Your Audience**: Build detailed audience avatars to clearly identify who you are designing for.

2. **Address Pain Points and Goals**: Align your course content with your audience's pain points and desired outcomes to create relevance and engagement.

3. **Resonate Emotionally and Intellectually**: Create content that both speaks to your audience's emotional journey and provides actionable, practical solutions.

4. **Gather Feedback**: Use surveys, conversations, and polls to gather insights before building your course, ensuring it directly addresses your audience's needs.

By deeply understanding your audience, you can create a course that doesn't just deliver content but delivers a transformative experience—one that feels personal, relevant, and worth investing in. In the next chapter, we'll dive into how to craft clear and inspiring course goals that keep your students motivated and excited to complete the journey.

CHAPTER 3:
Crafting Course Goals That Inspire

When Jessica first launched her course on mindfulness for busy professionals, she had high hopes. Her content was excellent, her presentations polished, and her audience seemed eager to learn. Yet, despite all her hard work, her students weren't finishing the course. She noticed a pattern in the feedback—many learners said they didn't feel clear on what they were supposed to achieve by the end of each module. The course was informative but lacked structure and direction. Determined to improve, Jessica went back to the drawing board and focused on rewriting her course goals. She transformed vague objectives like "understand mindfulness" into clear, actionable outcomes such as "learn how to incorporate a 5-minute mindfulness practice into your daily routine within 30 days." The results were immediate. With specific goals in place, students knew exactly what they were working toward and felt more motivated to complete the course. Completion rates soared, and Jessica's course became a bestseller in its niche.

The Power of Specific, Inspiring Course Goals

Jessica's story highlights an essential lesson in course creation: vague goals don't inspire action. In contrast, clear, specific, and inspiring course goals are the foundation of an engaging and successful course. These goals guide learners through their journey, providing them with a sense of purpose and direction from the first module to the last. Without well-defined goals, students can feel lost or unmotivated, unsure of what they should be focusing on or whether they are making progress. But when goals are actionable and tied to tangible outcomes, learners are more likely to stay engaged and complete the course.

In short, inspiring course goals not only frame the learner's experience but also provide a clear path to success.

Defining Clear, Achievable, and Motivating Course Goals

Crafting course goals that inspire requires more than just a general idea of what you want your students to learn. Your goals need to be specific, measurable, and aligned with the needs of your audience. Here's how you can define clear, achievable, and motivating course goals:

1. **Be Specific and Action-Oriented** A vague goal like "understand time management" doesn't give learners a concrete target to aim for. Instead, aim for something specific and action-oriented. For example, "Implement a daily time-blocking system to increase productivity within two weeks" is much clearer and more motivating. It tells learners not only

what they will achieve but *how* they will do it and by *when*.

2. **Make Goals Measurable** To keep learners motivated, it's important to give them a way to measure their progress. Avoid goals that are too abstract to track. Instead, use measurable outcomes like, "By the end of this module, you will have created a personalized fitness plan that fits your schedule," or "Complete a 30-day content calendar for your business." When learners can see concrete results from their efforts, it boosts their confidence and keeps them moving forward.

3. **Align Goals with Real-World Application** Learners are more likely to engage when they understand how the course will improve their personal or professional lives. Ensure your goals are tied to real-world outcomes that resonate with your audience's needs. For example, if your audience consists of entrepreneurs, a goal like "Increase your business's Instagram engagement by 20% in 30 days using actionable strategies" directly connects the course material with a tangible benefit.

4. **Break Down Goals by Module** Rather than having one overarching goal for the entire course, break down the learning objectives by module. This helps learners feel a sense of achievement throughout the course, rather than waiting until the end to see progress. For instance, Module 1's goal could be "Create a personal mission statement," while Module

2 might focus on "Identify three key areas of your business to streamline for efficiency."

5. **Keep Goals Realistic and Achievable** While it's important to challenge your students, setting unrealistic goals can backfire, leaving them frustrated or overwhelmed. Make sure each goal is attainable within the course's timeframe and skill level. For example, if your course is designed for beginners, don't set expert-level goals. Instead, provide a realistic progression, like "By the end of this course, you'll have mastered three beginner-level coding projects."

Aligning Goals with Audience Needs

In Chapter 2, we discussed the importance of understanding your audience's pain points and learning goals. Now, it's time to align your course goals with these needs. When learners feel that the course is tailored to their specific challenges and aspirations, they are more motivated to engage with the material and complete the course.

Here's how you can align your goals with audience needs:

1. **Identify the Transformation Your Audience Wants** Your learners are likely taking your course because they want to achieve a specific transformation—whether that's advancing their career, gaining a new skill, or solving a personal problem. Your course goals should reflect this desired transformation. For example, if your course is for busy professionals looking to reduce stress, a goal like "Develop a daily 10-minute meditation

practice to manage stress effectively" speaks directly to their needs.

2. **Create a Clear Path from Start to Finish** Course goals should provide a roadmap that guides learners from where they are now to where they want to be. Start with small, foundational goals that build confidence and lead into more complex or challenging objectives as the course progresses. This gradual progression helps learners stay engaged and prevents them from feeling overwhelmed. For example, in a course on personal finance, the first module might focus on "Setting up a simple monthly budget," while later modules work toward "Maximizing savings and investments."

3. **Consider Emotional and Practical Needs** Your course goals should address both the intellectual and emotional needs of your learners. For example, many students might be looking for practical skills but also need emotional reassurance that they can achieve these goals. Incorporate encouraging language and goals that build confidence along the way, such as "Gain the confidence to present your work to clients by learning effective communication strategies."

Crafting Goals that Promise Transformation

The most successful courses are those that promise a clear, tangible transformation. When learners sign up for a course, they're not just looking for information—they're looking for a change. Maybe they want to advance their career, improve their health, or start a business. Your course goals should clearly articulate how their lives will improve by the end of the program.

1. **Define the End Result** Start by defining the transformation your learners will experience. What will they be able to do differently after completing your course? How will their lives or careers be better? For example, instead of saying, "Learn how to use social media," aim for something more transformative, such as, "By the end of this course, you will have developed a personalized social media strategy that consistently attracts clients."

2. **Paint a Picture of Success** Use your course goals to paint a vivid picture of what success looks like. Rather than focusing on abstract skills, focus on the concrete results learners will achieve. For instance, in a course on productivity, a goal like, "By the end of this course, you will have implemented a daily routine that reduces your workweek by 10 hours" is much more compelling than "Learn time management."

Keeping Learners Motivated with a Clear Learning Path

Once you've crafted inspiring goals, it's important to ensure that learners can clearly see how they will achieve them. A clear learning path keeps students motivated by showing them how each module builds on the previous one and brings them closer to their desired transformation.

1. **Outline the Journey** Start your course by outlining the key goals for each module, so learners know

what to expect. Providing a roadmap at the beginning of the course helps students see the big picture and understand how each lesson is moving them toward their ultimate goal.

2. **Celebrate Milestones** Break the course into smaller sections and celebrate key milestones along the way. For example, after completing a module, remind learners of their progress: "Congratulations! You've just completed Module 3 and are now halfway to building your personal branding strategy." This keeps motivation high and gives learners a sense of achievement throughout the journey.

3. **Provide Feedback and Encouragement** Offering feedback, even in the form of automated quizzes or discussion prompts, helps learners gauge their progress toward the course goals. Positive reinforcement and reminders that they are on the right path will encourage them to keep moving forward.

Key Takeaways

Creating specific, clear, and inspiring course goals is essential for keeping learners engaged and motivated throughout the course. Here are the core principles to remember when crafting your course goals:

1. **Make Your Goals Specific and Measurable**: Clearly outline what learners will achieve by the end of each module and the course as a whole. Specificity gives learners a clear target to aim for.

2. **Align Goals with Audience Needs**: Tailor your course goals to the transformation your audience is seeking, ensuring that the outcomes resonate with their personal or professional aspirations.

3. **Promise Transformation**: Focus on crafting goals that promise real, tangible changes in the learner's life or career, making the course feel worthwhile.

4. **Provide a Clear Learning Path**: Guide learners through their journey with well-defined goals for each stage, and celebrate milestones along the way to keep motivation high.

By taking the time to craft course goals that inspire and motivate, you set the stage for a learning experience that engages students from start to finish. In the next chapter, we'll explore how to build interactive and dynamic learning experiences that keep learners engaged every step of the way.

CHAPTER 4:
Building Interactive and Dynamic Learning

When Leah created her first course on leadership skills for emerging female entrepreneurs, she struggled to keep her students engaged. Despite her deep knowledge and compelling content, her learners were dropping off midway through the course. Determined to find a solution, Leah decided to revamp her course by making it more interactive. She added live Q&A sessions, incorporated real-life leadership scenarios where students had to make decisions, and implemented interactive quizzes at the end of each module. The transformation was remarkable—her students not only stayed engaged until the very last module, but they also raved about how dynamic and immersive the experience was. By making her course interactive, Leah created an experience that felt hands-on and alive, rather than passive.

Why Engagement Requires Thoughtful Interaction

Leah's success story highlights an important truth about online learning: engagement requires more than just delivering information—it requires thoughtful, well-designed interaction. The days of students passively watching video lectures and then moving on are over. Today's learners want to feel involved, like they are a part of the learning process. To create a high-value course that holds students' attention from start to finish, you need to build in opportunities for them to *do*, not just *watch*.

Interactive learning transforms passive participants into active learners, giving them the tools to engage deeply with the material. When students feel involved, they are more likely to stay motivated, retain information, and apply what they've learned. In this chapter, we'll explore the blueprint for building engaging, interactive courses that captivate learners and keep them coming back for more.

Tools and Strategies for Creating Interaction

Interactive learning doesn't happen by accident—it's the result of deliberate planning and the use of specific tools and strategies that invite learners to participate in their education. Let's explore some of the most effective methods to create interaction within your course.

1. Quizzes and Knowledge Checks

Quizzes are one of the simplest and most effective ways to create interaction. They allow learners to test their understanding of the material in real-time, reinforcing key concepts and giving them immediate feedback. You can incorporate quizzes at the end of each module or after critical lessons to ensure that learners are grasping the content before moving on.

Pro Tip: Use a mix of question types—multiple-choice, true/false, and scenario-based questions—to keep quizzes interesting and challenging. For example, after teaching a module on personal branding, ask, "Which of the following elements is most crucial for establishing a strong personal brand?" followed by scenario-based questions that apply the concepts.

2. Group Work and Collaboration

People learn well when they work together, so incorporating group activities into your course can enhance engagement. Assign students to small groups where they can collaborate on projects, share ideas, and solve problems together. Group discussions can take place in forums, private messaging platforms, or even through live virtual meetings.

Pro Tip: In a course on entrepreneurship, you might ask groups to brainstorm business ideas based on case studies, then present their ideas to the rest of the class in a live session. This encourages peer learning and gives students the chance to practice critical thinking and communication skills.

3. Live Sessions and Webinars

Live sessions allow students to interact with you in real-time, asking questions, sharing insights, and engaging in discussions. This creates a sense of immediacy and personal connection that prerecorded content can't match. You can host live Q&A sessions, guest expert interviews, or interactive webinars that dive deeper into course content.

Pro Tip: Schedule live sessions at key points in the course, such as after completing a major module or before starting the final project. This creates a natural point of reflection and offers students a chance to clarify concepts or seek advice before moving forward.

4. Interactive Videos

Interactive videos take traditional video content to the next level by allowing students to make choices, answer questions, or engage in scenarios directly within the video. This keeps learners actively engaged, as they must respond to prompts rather than passively watching the content.

Pro Tip: If you're teaching a course on leadership, you could create an interactive video where students choose how to handle a challenging leadership scenario, then receive tailored feedback based on their choices. This makes the learning experience more immersive and practical.

5. Discussions and Community Engagement

Online discussions and forums give learners a place to engage with their peers, ask questions, and share their thoughts on the material. Building a community around your course can significantly increase engagement, as students feel a sense of belonging and accountability when they interact with others on the same journey.

Pro Tip: Set up a dedicated forum or private Facebook group where learners can discuss course material, share experiences, and ask for help. Regularly participate in the discussions to keep the conversation going and to build a stronger connection with your students.

Incorporating Storytelling and Scenarios to Deepen Engagement

Storytelling is one of the most powerful ways to engage learners emotionally and intellectually. When you tell stories or create real-life scenarios, you bring your content to life in a way that resonates with students and makes abstract concepts easier to understand. Stories help learners see how the material applies to their lives, and scenarios allow them to practice applying their knowledge in realistic situations.

1. Case Studies and Real-Life Examples

Using case studies and real-world examples helps students see the practical application of what they're learning. Share stories from your own experience or use examples from your industry to illustrate key points. For example, in a course on public speaking, you could share a story about how one of your students overcame stage fright by using specific techniques you teach.

Pro Tip: Incorporate a "learn by doing" approach by asking learners to analyze a case study and make decisions based on the scenario, followed by a discussion on their choices and outcomes.

2. Role-Playing and Simulations

Role-playing and simulations allow learners to step into different roles and practice their skills in a safe, controlled environment. This can be especially effective in courses that teach soft skills, like communication or conflict resolution.

Pro Tip: In a course on negotiation, for instance, you could create role-playing exercises where students practice negotiating deals, then reflect on what strategies worked and what didn't. This kind of interactive learning is both engaging and practical, helping learners build real-world skills.

Using Gamification to Make Learning Fun and Sticky

Gamification refers to applying game-like elements to your course to make learning more fun, engaging, and motivating. It taps into learners' natural desire for achievement, competition, and recognition, which keeps them motivated to progress through the course.

1. Badges and Rewards

Awarding badges or certificates for completing certain milestones—such as finishing a module or scoring well on a quiz—adds an element of achievement to the course. Learners can collect badges as they go, which provides them with a sense of accomplishment.

Pro Tip: Create different levels of badges that correlate with specific goals. For instance, you could have a "Problem Solver" badge for completing all the quizzes with a high score or a "Team Player" badge for actively participating in group work.

2. Leaderboards

Leaderboards create healthy competition by allowing students to see how they rank compared to their peers. This can be especially motivating for learners who thrive on competition or want to challenge themselves to do better.

Pro Tip: You can rank students based on quiz scores, participation in discussions, or even the speed at which they complete course milestones. Make sure to balance competition with encouragement to ensure a positive learning environment.

3. Progress Tracking

Allow learners to track their progress throughout the course with visual indicators like progress bars or completion percentages. This provides them with a clear sense of where they are in their learning journey and motivates them to keep going until they reach 100%.

Pro Tip: Include small celebrations when students complete milestones, like congratulatory messages or unlocking bonus content, to keep the experience positive and rewarding.

Key Takeaways

By incorporating interactivity and dynamic elements into your course, you can transform the learning experience from passive to deeply engaging. Here are the key tools and strategies for building an interactive and dynamic course:

1. **Use Quizzes and Knowledge Checks**: Keep learners engaged and on track by regularly testing their understanding of the material.

2. **Incorporate Group Work and Live Sessions**: Create opportunities for collaboration and real-time interaction to foster engagement and community.

3. **Add Interactive Videos and Storytelling**: Bring your content to life with interactive scenarios, real-world examples, and immersive storytelling.

4. **Leverage Gamification**: Use badges, leaderboards, and progress tracking to make learning fun, competitive, and rewarding.

By using these tools and methods, you can build an engaging course that keeps learners motivated, active, and eager to reach the finish line. In the next chapter, we'll dive into the importance of design and aesthetics in enhancing your course's perceived value and keeping your learners hooked from the moment they sign up.

CHAPTER 5:
Enhancing Perceived Value with Visual and Emotional Design

When Rachel first launched her course on time management for working moms, she had excellent content. Her lessons were practical, insightful, and full of actionable advice. But her students weren't sticking around to finish the course. She couldn't figure out why—until she realized that the course's presentation was lackluster. The interface was cluttered, the branding was inconsistent, and the visuals didn't align with the quality of her content. Determined to turn things around, Rachel invested in a clean, professional course layout, improved her branding, and added emotionally resonant imagery that spoke to her audience. Almost immediately, the feedback improved. Learners felt more connected to the course, engaged more deeply with the material, and completion rates soared. The content was the same, but the visual and emotional design made all the difference.

Design Matters: How Presentation Influences Perceived Value

Rachel's story illustrates a critical point: **design matters**. In the world of online learning, presentation plays a massive role in how students perceive the value of your course. Even if your content is high quality, poor design can make it seem less credible, confusing, or unprofessional. On the other hand, a well-designed course can elevate your content, making it feel polished, trustworthy, and worth the investment.

When learners first encounter your course, they aren't just judging the material—they're also evaluating how it *looks* and *feels*. From the layout and branding to the flow of the content, every design element impacts how learners experience your course. A cohesive, professional design helps establish trust and credibility, while an emotionally resonant aesthetic connects learners on a deeper level. Together, these design principles create a learning environment that feels not only educational but also enriching and motivating.

Best Practices for Designing a Visually Appealing Course Interface

Designing a visually appealing course doesn't require advanced design skills—it just requires a thoughtful approach to the elements that shape the learner's experience. Here are some best practices to create a visually stunning course interface:

1. **Simplicity and Clarity** A cluttered, complicated interface overwhelms learners and makes it difficult to focus on the material. Instead, aim for simplicity.

Ensure that your course platform is clean, with clear navigation and minimal distractions. Use plenty of white space to give learners breathing room and to direct their attention to what's most important.

Pro Tip: Stick to a limited color palette—usually 2-3 complementary colors—so the design feels cohesive without being overpowering. Consistency across your design creates a sense of professionalism.

2. **Readable Typography** The fonts you use in your course can have a significant impact on readability and overall aesthetic. Choose fonts that are easy to read on screens and that align with your branding. Avoid overly decorative or complex fonts, which can make reading difficult and frustrate learners.

Pro Tip: Use a hierarchy in your typography by choosing different font sizes for headings, subheadings, and body text. This helps guide learners' eyes through the content and improves comprehension.

3. **Consistent Branding** Your branding should be consistent throughout your course. From the colors and fonts you use to your logo and imagery, maintaining a cohesive brand presence reinforces your professionalism and helps build trust with your learners.

Pro Tip: Create a style guide that includes your brand colors, fonts, and logo placement to ensure consistency across all course materials.

4. **Visual Hierarchy** Organize your content in a way that visually guides learners through the course. Use

headings, subheadings, bullet points, and numbered lists to break up long sections of text and make the content easier to digest. This makes your course not only more visually appealing but also more navigable.

Pro Tip: Use visuals, such as icons or images, to highlight key points or important sections of your course. This helps draw attention to crucial information and enhances the learning experience.

Building Emotional Resonance Through Design

In addition to looking good, your course should also *feel* good. Emotional resonance is what keeps learners connected to your content on a deeper level. By integrating elements that evoke emotion—whether through storytelling, visual elements, or course layout—you can create a stronger connection with your audience.

1. **Storytelling and Visuals** As humans, we're wired to respond to stories. Incorporating storytelling into your course, through both words and visuals, helps create an emotional connection with learners. Whether it's sharing personal anecdotes or using visuals that evoke a specific feeling, storytelling makes the content more relatable and engaging.

Pro Tip: Use images and videos that reflect the emotions and aspirations of your target audience. For example, if your course is about empowering women in business, choose visuals that show confident, successful women in professional settings.

2. **Color Psychology** The colors you use in your course can subtly influence how learners feel. Certain colors evoke specific emotions—blue can inspire trust and calm, while red can stimulate excitement or urgency. Be intentional about your color choices and use them to reinforce the emotions you want learners to feel.

Pro Tip: Use calming colors like blue or green in sections where learners need to focus, and brighter colors like orange or red to highlight calls to action or important announcements.

3. **Layout that Flows** The layout of your course should feel intuitive and seamless. When learners move from one module to the next, the transitions should feel natural. Avoid overwhelming students with too much content at once; instead, break it up into manageable chunks that allow them to absorb and reflect on the material.

Pro Tip: Use a modular layout, where each section or module is self-contained but flows logically into the next. This helps maintain a sense of progression and achievement as learners move through the course.

Creating a Cohesive, Professional Aesthetic that Boosts Credibility

A cohesive, professional aesthetic isn't just about making your course *look* good—it's about building *trust*. When learners see a polished, well-designed course, they're more likely to believe in the quality of the content and the credibility of the instructor. A consistent design shows that you've put thought and care into every aspect of the course, which in turn signals to learners that they're in good hands.

1. **Align Visuals with Your Brand's Tone** If your brand is lighthearted and fun, your course design should reflect that with bright colors, playful fonts, and lively imagery. If your brand is more serious and professional, a sleek, modern design with minimalistic elements might be more appropriate. Make sure that the visuals in your course align with the overall tone and message of your brand.

2. **Invest in High-Quality Visuals** High-quality visuals—whether photos, illustrations, or graphics—add a layer of professionalism to your course. Avoid using generic stock photos or low-quality images, as they can cheapen the overall experience. Instead, invest in visuals that are unique, clear, and aligned with your brand's identity.

Pro Tip: If hiring a designer isn't an option, use tools like Canva or Adobe Spark, which provide templates and resources to create professional-quality visuals with ease.

3. **Leverage Video for Personal Connection** Videos are one of the most powerful tools for building a personal connection with your learners. Recording short introduction videos for each module or including video-based lessons can make your course feel more dynamic and engaging. Make sure that your videos are well-lit, clearly recorded, and professionally edited to maintain a high level of quality.

Pro Tip: Use video strategically to build rapport with your audience—especially in the first few modules—so learners feel connected to you as their instructor.

Key Takeaways

Design is about more than aesthetics—it's about creating a course experience that looks great, feels engaging, and enhances perceived value. Here's how you can boost your course's visual and emotional design:

1. **Simplicity and Clarity**: Keep your course layout clean and easy to navigate, using plenty of white space and a limited color palette.

2. **Emotional Resonance**: Use storytelling, imagery, and color psychology to build a deeper emotional connection with learners.

3. **Consistency and Branding**: Maintain a cohesive design that reflects your brand's tone and values across all materials and platforms.

4. **Invest in High-Quality Visuals**: Use professional-quality images, graphics, and videos to enhance the overall look and feel of your course.

By paying attention to both visual and emotional design, you can elevate your course from "good" to "great," making it a high-perceived value experience that leaves a lasting impression on your learners. In the next chapter, we'll explore how to market and position your course to maximize enrollment and revenue.

CHAPTER 6:
Positioning and Marketing Your High-Value Course

When Amelia launched her online course on digital photography, she had a solid product with well-structured content and visually appealing lessons. But despite the value it offered, her course wasn't selling. She knew it wasn't a lack of demand—plenty of people were interested in learning photography—but somehow, her message wasn't cutting through the noise. Determined to figure it out, Amelia focused on repositioning her course. She reworked her marketing to emphasize the transformation her students would experience—going from amateur photographers to confident, sought-after professionals. She also leveraged testimonials from past students, highlighting real success stories. Almost overnight, things shifted. Her course went from struggling to sold out in just a few weeks. What changed? The course was the same—but the *positioning* transformed everything.

The Power of Positioning: How Marketing Impacts Perceived Value

Amelia's story highlights an essential truth about selling online courses: the way you *position* and market your course can be the difference between a lackluster launch and a sold-out success. Even the most valuable course won't sell if it isn't marketed effectively. Your audience needs to see, clearly and immediately, why your course is the *must-have* solution to their problems. In today's crowded online education space, your ability to communicate your course's unique value—what makes it different and better—determines your success.

Perceived value starts long before students log in for the first lesson. It begins the moment they land on your sales page, read your course description, or hear about your offering. This is why *positioning* matters so much. Your course may be packed with value, but if you don't position it properly in your marketing, you'll struggle to convince potential students to invest in it.

Identifying Your Unique Selling Proposition (USP)

The first step to positioning your course as a must-have solution is identifying your **Unique Selling Proposition (USP)**. Your USP is the unique value that sets your course apart from the competition. It answers the key question: *Why should someone choose your course over others?*

Here's how to identify your USP:

1. **Focus on Transformation**: What transformation will your students experience after completing your course? This is often the most compelling aspect of your USP. For example, Amelia repositioned her

photography course by emphasizing how her students would go from hobbyists to confident professionals with a portfolio of work by the end of the course.

2. **Highlight What Makes Your Approach Unique**: Maybe it's your teaching style, your background, or the interactive elements you've built into your course. Find what differentiates your course from others in the market. Are you offering a more hands-on experience? Do you provide more personal feedback or unique content that no one else does?

3. **Address Your Audience's Specific Needs**: Your USP should align with the specific challenges and goals of your target audience. What pain points are they struggling with that your course solves? For example, Amelia's USP addressed the fear and uncertainty that amateur photographers felt about going pro.

Once you've identified your USP, it becomes the foundation of all your marketing efforts. Every piece of content you create—from your course description to your emails and social media posts—should clearly communicate the unique value your course offers.

Crafting Irresistible Course Descriptions That Focus on Transformation

One of the most critical pieces of your marketing is your **course description**. This is often the first thing potential students will read, and it's your chance to grab their attention and convince them that your course is the solution they've been searching for.

Here's how to craft a compelling course description:

1. **Lead with the Transformation**: Don't start with a list of features or the number of modules your course includes. Instead, lead with the *transformation* your students will experience. Paint a picture of what life will look like for them after completing your course. For example, rather than saying, "This course covers advanced photography techniques," you might say, "By the end of this course, you'll have the skills and confidence to take professional-quality photos that wow your clients."

2. **Speak to Their Pain Points**: A great course description addresses your audience's struggles. What's keeping them up at night? What problem are they desperate to solve? Acknowledge their pain points and show them how your course will help them overcome these challenges.

3. **Outline Clear Outcomes**: Be specific about what your students will walk away with. For example, "By the end of this course, you'll have built a professional portfolio, mastered editing techniques, and developed a personal style that sets you apart in the photography industry." Clear, tangible outcomes help potential students visualize the value they'll receive.

4. **Use Engaging, Emotion-Driven Language**: Remember, you're not just selling a course—you're

selling a *dream*. Use emotionally charged language to convey the excitement, confidence, or success that your course will help your students achieve. For example, "Imagine having the confidence to turn your passion into a thriving photography business."

Leveraging Testimonials and Social Proof to Build Trust

One of the most effective ways to boost the perceived value of your course is through **testimonials and social proof**. People are more likely to invest in a course if they see that others have taken it and had a positive experience. Testimonials build trust and credibility, showing potential students that your course delivers on its promises.

Here's how to effectively leverage testimonials:

1. **Collect Success Stories**: Reach out to your past students and ask for specific testimonials about how your course helped them achieve their goals. Instead of vague feedback like "This course was great," aim for detailed stories: "Before taking this course, I struggled with time management in my business. Now, I've implemented the strategies I learned, and my productivity has doubled."

2. **Use Visuals**: Wherever possible, include a photo of the student along with their testimonial. This makes the feedback feel more personal and authentic. If they're willing, ask students to share video testimonials, which are even more powerful.

3. **Highlight Key Metrics or Results**: If your students achieved measurable results from your

course, make sure to include that in their testimonials. For example, "After implementing what I learned, I increased my monthly sales by 50%."

4. **Feature Testimonials Prominently**: Display testimonials on your sales page, within your email marketing, and on social media. Social proof should be a central part of your marketing strategy, as it reassures potential students that your course is worth the investment.

Positioning Your Course as the Must-Have Solution

Now that you've identified your USP and crafted compelling course descriptions, it's time to position your course as the *must-have* solution. This means clearly communicating the value of your course in a way that makes it feel like the obvious choice for your target audience.

Here's how to position your course effectively:

1. **Create a Sense of Urgency**: Encourage potential students to act quickly by incorporating deadlines or limited-time offers. For example, "Enroll before [date] to receive a 20% discount" or "Only 50 spots available in this live coaching program—secure your place today!" Creating urgency helps drive action and prevents procrastination.

2. **Emphasize Scarcity**: If your course includes live elements, one-on-one coaching, or limited spots, make it clear that space is limited. Scarcity increases the perceived value and encourages students to act before it's too late.

3. **Offer Bonuses**: Sweeten the deal by offering exclusive bonuses for students who enroll by a certain date. This could include bonus content, one-on-one coaching sessions, or downloadable resources. Bonuses add extra value and make students feel like they're getting more for their money.

4. **Use Strong Calls to Action (CTAs)**: Your marketing should always include clear and compelling calls to action that guide potential students toward enrollment. Instead of saying "Sign up now," use action-driven language like "Start your transformation today" or "Unlock the skills you need to build your dream business."

Crafting Sales Copy That Converts

To truly sell the dream, your sales copy needs to be compelling, clear, and conversion-focused. Here are some tips for writing sales copy that turns interested readers into paying students:

1. **Focus on Benefits, Not Features**: Instead of listing out every feature of your course, focus on the benefits. What's in it for the student? How will their life improve? For example, instead of "Includes 10 video lessons," say, "Master the art of copywriting with 10 easy-to-follow video lessons that teach you proven techniques."

2. **Tell a Story**: Stories are powerful tools for connecting with your audience. Share a personal story of how you learned the concepts in your

course or tell the success story of a past student who achieved incredible results. Stories humanize your marketing and make your course feel relatable.

3. **Create a Clear and Easy-to-Navigate Sales Page**: Your sales page should be clean, professional, and easy to navigate. Break the text into sections with clear headings, bullet points, and visuals that guide the reader through the benefits of the course and the enrollment process.

4. **End with a Strong CTA**: Always conclude your sales copy with a clear, actionable call to action. Tell potential students exactly what they need to do next to enroll, and remind them of the benefits they'll receive by taking action now.

Key Takeaways

Selling your course is about more than just listing what it offers—it's about selling the *dream* and positioning it as the must-have solution. Here's how to effectively market and position your course:

1. **Identify Your USP**: Focus on what sets your course apart and the transformation it offers.

2. **Craft Compelling Course Descriptions**: Lead with the transformation your students will experience, and speak to their pain points and goals.

3. **Leverage Testimonials and Social Proof**: Use past success stories and real results to build trust and credibility.

4. **Create a Sense of Urgency and Scarcity**: Encourage potential students to act quickly by highlighting limited availability and offering exclusive bonuses.

By focusing on positioning, you can transform a good course into a sold-out success. In the next chapter, we'll explore pricing strategies that reflect your course's value and help you maximize your revenue.

CHAPTER 7:
Pricing for Profit and Value

When Sophia first launched her online course on social media marketing, she priced it at $99. She figured a lower price would attract more students and make her course more accessible. But despite having a well-structured course and solid content, her sales were underwhelming. After receiving feedback from a business coach, she decided to take a risk—she raised her course price to $499 and added a few premium features, like personalized coaching calls and a private mastermind group. To her surprise, her sales skyrocketed. Not only did she attract more students, but they were also more engaged and committed to completing the course. What happened? Sophia realized that her original pricing sent the wrong message about the value of her course. By increasing the price, she signaled that the course was high-quality, exclusive, and worth the investment.

Pricing Communicates Value: Why Pricing Matters

Sophia's story demonstrates a crucial lesson in online course creation: **pricing communicates value**. How you price your course is one of the most important decisions you'll make, because it affects how potential students perceive your offering. Many course creators, especially first-timers, make the mistake of pricing their courses too low in an effort to attract more students. But what they don't realize is that low prices can often send the message that the course isn't valuable or comprehensive enough to justify a higher price tag.

Pricing is more than just a number; it's a psychological signal that tells potential students what they can expect from your course. A higher price suggests premium content, expert-level instruction, and a transformative learning experience. On the flip side, a low price can imply that the course is basic or introductory, even if it's packed with valuable insights. The key is to strike the right balance between **profitability** and **perceived value**.

The Psychology of Pricing: Why Charging More Can Increase Perceived Value

Pricing isn't just about covering your costs or setting a price that feels "fair"—it's about understanding the psychology of how people perceive value. Let's explore some of the key principles behind pricing psychology:

1. **Higher Prices Signal Higher Value** In many cases, people assume that a higher price means higher quality. This is especially true in the world of online courses, where there's a wide range of pricing

options. When potential students see a course priced at $50 next to one priced at $500, they'll often assume that the higher-priced course offers more in-depth, expert-level content. Higher prices signal to learners that they're making an investment in their education, which can increase their commitment to the course.

Pro Tip: If you have a high-value course that delivers transformational outcomes, don't be afraid to price it accordingly. Your price should reflect the value and results that your students will achieve.

2. **Perceived Exclusivity Drives Demand** When something feels exclusive or limited, people are more likely to want it. Pricing your course higher creates a sense of exclusivity, signaling that this isn't just any course—it's a premium learning experience. This is particularly effective when combined with limited availability (such as a capped number of students per cohort) or personalized support.

Pro Tip: You can further increase the perceived exclusivity by offering premium add-ons like one-on-one coaching, private mastermind groups, or direct access to you as the instructor.

3. **Pricing Affects Commitment** Students who pay more for a course are often more committed to completing it. When people invest a significant amount of money, they're more likely to take the course seriously, put in the effort, and stay engaged. On the other hand, low-priced courses are often

seen as less important, and students may not feel as motivated to finish.

Pro Tip: Price your course at a level that reflects the effort and results you expect from your students. Higher prices can help attract serious, motivated learners who are ready to commit to their growth.

Balancing Affordability and Profitability

While pricing higher can increase perceived value, it's important to strike the right balance between affordability and profitability. You want your course to be accessible to your target audience, but you also need to ensure that it reflects the value you're offering and supports your business goals.

1. **Know Your Audience's Willingness to Pay** Understanding your target audience's budget and willingness to pay is critical. If you're targeting seasoned professionals or entrepreneurs, they may be willing to invest more in a course that will advance their career or business. However, if your audience consists of beginners or individuals in a more price-sensitive market, you may need to adjust your pricing accordingly.

Pro Tip: Survey your audience or do market research to gauge how much they're willing to spend on a course like yours. This will give you insight into pricing levels that feel both valuable and accessible to your students.

2. **Tiered Pricing Options** One way to balance affordability and profitability is by offering **tiered pricing**. This allows you to create different levels of

access or content, giving students more options based on their budget and needs. For example:

- **Basic Tier**: Access to the core course content (e.g., video lessons, downloadable resources).
- **Mid-Tier**: Includes everything in the Basic Tier, plus additional features like live Q&A sessions, group coaching, or extra modules.
- **Premium Tier**: Includes all lower-tier features plus exclusive perks like one-on-one coaching, a personalized action plan, or lifetime access to course updates.

Pro Tip: Tiered pricing allows you to capture different segments of your audience, increasing your overall revenue while still offering affordable options.

3. **Offering Payment Plans** Another way to make higher-priced courses more accessible is by offering **payment plans**. This can reduce the upfront financial burden for students while still allowing you to maintain a profitable price point. For example, if your course costs $1,000, you could offer a payment plan of $250/month for four months.

Pro Tip: Payment plans can also encourage students to commit to your higher-priced offerings, as they feel more manageable when broken down into smaller payments.

Offering Tiered Pricing or Premium Packages

One of the most effective ways to increase revenue and provide more value to your students is by offering **premium**

packages or **tiered pricing**. By creating different levels of access, you can offer something for everyone—from budget-conscious students to those looking for a high-end, exclusive experience.

1. **Basic, Standard, and Premium Tiers** By offering multiple tiers, you give potential students options based on their needs and budget. For example:
   - **Basic Tier**: Access to essential course content, ideal for students looking for an introduction to the subject.
   - **Standard Tier**: Includes the core content plus additional features like group coaching sessions or live Q&A.
   - **Premium Tier**: Full access, including one-on-one coaching, personalized feedback, and lifetime updates.

Pro Tip: Emphasize the value of each tier in your marketing materials, showing students what extra benefits they'll receive at higher levels. This creates a natural incentive for students to choose the more expensive option.

2. **Add-On Packages** Another option is to offer **add-ons** that students can purchase separately. For example, if your course covers digital marketing, you could offer an add-on package with personalized website audits, one-on-one strategy sessions, or additional resources like templates and guides.

Pro Tip: Make sure that your add-on packages provide significant value beyond the core course. These extras should feel like a natural extension of the course and offer additional transformation or insights.

Maximizing Profit While Maintaining High Perceived Value

Once you've decided on your pricing structure, it's important to ensure that you're maximizing profit while maintaining the perceived value of your course. Here are some strategies to achieve this balance:

1. **Raise Prices Gradually** If you're worried about pricing too high from the start, consider raising your prices gradually. As you gain testimonials, refine your course, and establish yourself as an authority in your field, you can confidently raise your prices over time. This allows you to test the market and adjust your pricing strategy based on demand and feedback.

2. **Offer Limited-Time Discounts** Offering limited-time discounts or early-bird pricing can create a sense of urgency and drive sales. However, be careful not to rely on discounts too heavily, as they can sometimes lower the perceived value of your course. Instead, use them strategically for new launches or special promotions.

3. **Communicate the Value Clearly** No matter how you price your course, it's essential to clearly communicate the value it provides. Break down the benefits, outcomes, and transformation your students will experience. Use testimonials, success

stories, and clear descriptions of what students will gain to justify your price point.

Key Takeaways

Pricing your course is about more than just choosing a number—it's about positioning your course in a way that reflects its value and appeals to your target audience. Here's how to price your course for profit and perceived value:

1. **Understand Pricing Psychology**: Higher prices signal higher value and exclusivity, and can lead to more committed students.

2. **Balance Affordability and Profitability**: Know your audience's budget, offer tiered pricing, and consider payment plans to make your course more accessible while maximizing revenue.

3. **Use Tiered Pricing and Add-On Packages**: Offer different pricing tiers or add-on packages to give students more options and boost your earnings.

4. **Communicate the Value**: Ensure that your pricing is backed up by clear, compelling messaging that highlights the benefits and outcomes of your course.

By pricing your course confidently and strategically, you'll not only increase your revenue but also enhance the perceived value of your course, attracting serious students who are ready to invest in their own transformation. In the next chapter, we'll explore how to create an ongoing support system that keeps your students engaged long after the course ends.

CHAPTER 8:
Building a Supportive Community

When Mia launched her first course on mindfulness and stress management, she expected her content to do the heavy lifting. But something unexpected happened—her students weren't just completing the lessons, they were forming connections with one another. After seeing how much her learners enjoyed interacting, Mia decided to formalize a community around her course. She created a private Facebook group where students could share experiences, ask questions, and offer support. Soon, that community took on a life of its own, with members organizing their own accountability groups, sharing personal victories, and even collaborating on side projects. Mia realized that the community she built became one of the most valuable aspects of her course. Students who might have otherwise disengaged found motivation and support from their peers, increasing completion rates and driving loyalty to Mia's brand.

Why Community Matters: Enhancing Learning and Increasing Value

Mia's experience illustrates a key point in online course creation: **community enhances learning and increases perceived value**. While your content provides the foundation, a supportive community keeps learners engaged, encourages deeper learning, and builds a sense of belonging that lasts long after the final module. A thriving community adds tremendous value to your course, turning it into more than just a transaction—it becomes an experience that fosters connection, growth, and loyalty.

When learners feel like they're part of a community, they're more likely to stay committed to the course, complete it, and even return for future offerings. Community builds trust, provides accountability, and creates an environment where learners can ask questions, get feedback, and share insights. For many students, this level of engagement is what sets your course apart from others, adding another layer of value that helps justify a premium price tag.

How to Build and Manage a Thriving Community

Building a community around your course doesn't happen by accident—it requires intention, structure, and ongoing management. Here's how to create and manage a supportive community that enhances learning:

1. **Choose the Right Platform** The first step in building a community is choosing the platform where your learners will gather. Popular options include Facebook Groups, private forums (like those hosted on platforms such as Circle or Mighty

Networks), or even Slack or Discord channels. Your platform choice should align with the preferences of your audience and the type of engagement you want to foster.

Pro Tip: Facebook Groups are popular for their ease of use and familiarity, but if you want to create a more exclusive or focused community, consider a paid platform like Mighty Networks, which offers more features for community-building and engagement.

2. **Set Clear Expectations and Guidelines** To create a positive, engaging space, it's important to establish clear expectations and community guidelines from the beginning. Let your students know what kind of behavior is expected, how they should interact with one another, and the types of discussions that are encouraged. This helps create a safe and respectful environment where everyone feels welcome.

Pro Tip: Pin a welcome post at the top of your group or community forum with rules, guidelines, and an introduction. This ensures that new members know how to get involved and what's expected of them.

3. **Facilitate Discussions and Engagement** As the course creator, it's your job to facilitate conversations and keep the community active—especially in the early stages. Post regularly to spark discussions, ask thought-provoking questions, and encourage students to share their experiences or challenges. The more active you are in the

community, the more likely your students are to engage.

Pro Tip: Create daily or weekly prompts that encourage participation. For example, in a business coaching course, you might have "Motivation Mondays" where students share their goals for the week and "Feedback Fridays" where they discuss what worked well and what they struggled with.

4. **Incorporate Live Events** Live events, such as Q&A sessions, workshops, or group coaching calls, can create a sense of immediacy and personal connection within your community. These events give students direct access to you and allow them to engage with each other in real-time. Live events not only keep students engaged but also provide opportunities for deeper learning and peer interaction.

Pro Tip: Host monthly or bi-weekly live events where students can ask questions, share their progress, and get feedback from you and their peers. This can be done via Zoom or through live streams in your community platform.

5. **Encourage Peer Learning and Networking** One of the biggest benefits of having a community is the opportunity for peer learning and networking. Encourage your students to share their knowledge, collaborate on projects, and support each other's goals. Peer learning creates a more dynamic, interactive environment where students feel invested in each other's success.

Pro Tip: Assign accountability partners or small peer groups within your community. This gives students a chance to connect more deeply, stay motivated, and work through challenges together.

6. **Provide Ongoing Value** For your community to thrive long-term, it's important to provide ongoing value even after the course ends. This could include sharing new resources, offering exclusive content or bonus lessons, or running alumni events. By continuing to offer value, you give your students a reason to stay engaged and connected with your course—and with you.

Pro Tip: Offer lifetime access to your community as part of the course package. This gives students the opportunity to stay involved, network with future cohorts, and access ongoing support.

Tools and Platforms for Building an Engaging Learning Community

Choosing the right tools and platforms is crucial to building an effective learning community. Here are some of the most popular and effective options for creating and managing your course community:

1. **Facebook Groups**: Facebook Groups are one of the most common platforms for building course communities. They're easy to set up, familiar to most users, and offer a wide range of engagement features like live video, polls, and group chats. Plus, Facebook's algorithm helps keep active groups visible in users' feeds, encouraging participation.

2. **Mighty Networks**: Mighty Networks is a paid platform that allows you to create a more exclusive, branded community. It's great for course creators who want to offer a premium experience with features like event hosting, member profiles, and paid memberships.

3. **Slack**: Slack is ideal for more business-oriented or professional communities. Its channel-based structure makes it easy to organize discussions by topic, and it integrates with other tools like Google Drive, Trello, and Zoom for seamless collaboration.

4. **Discord**: Originally designed for gaming communities, Discord has grown into a popular option for all types of online communities. Its real-time chat features and voice channels make it ideal for courses with a younger audience or those focused on tech or creative industries.

5. **Circle**: Circle is a premium platform designed specifically for building course communities. It offers a clean, professional interface, and integrates well with popular course platforms like Teachable and Thinkific.

Practical Tips for Building a Learning Community That Lasts

Creating a community is just the first step—keeping it active and engaged over time is the real challenge. Here are some practical tips for building a community that lasts:

1. **Be Consistent**: Consistency is key to maintaining an active community. Post regularly, respond to

comments, and check in with your students frequently. The more active you are, the more engaged your community will be.

2. **Celebrate Wins and Milestones**: Recognize and celebrate the achievements of your students, whether it's completing a module, landing a new client, or reaching a personal goal. Publicly acknowledging these wins fosters a positive, supportive atmosphere and encourages others to stay engaged.

3. **Foster Relationships**: Encourage students to connect with each other on a personal level. Whether it's through accountability partnerships, small group discussions, or networking events, the relationships they build with their peers will keep them engaged long after the course ends.

4. **Use Gamification**: Incorporate gamification elements like badges, points, or leaderboards to make participation in the community more fun and motivating. Gamification rewards active members and encourages friendly competition, which can boost overall engagement.

5. **Solicit Feedback**: Regularly ask your community members for feedback on what's working and what could be improved. Listening to your students and making adjustments based on their feedback will help you build a stronger, more engaged community.

Key Takeaways

Building a supportive community around your course enhances the learning experience, increases perceived value, and creates long-lasting engagement. Here's how to create a thriving community that adds value to your course:

1. **Choose the Right Platform**: Select a platform that fits your audience's needs and makes it easy for them to engage with you and each other.

2. **Facilitate Engagement**: Regularly post discussion prompts, facilitate live events, and encourage peer interaction to keep the community active and engaged.

3. **Foster Peer Learning**: Encourage students to learn from each other through collaboration, networking, and accountability partnerships.

4. **Provide Ongoing Value**: Keep the community active even after the course ends by offering continued support, new content, and opportunities for alumni to connect.

By fostering a supportive community, you not only increase the value of your course but also create a space where learners feel connected, motivated, and empowered to achieve their goals. In the next chapter, we'll explore how to offer ongoing support and course optimization to ensure your students' success well beyond their initial enrollment.

CHAPTER 9:
Ongoing Support and Course Optimization

When Karen launched her online course on graphic design for beginners, it was a hit. The first cohort sold out within weeks, and the feedback was overwhelmingly positive. But instead of resting on her success, Karen focused on supporting her students beyond the initial course and continuously improving the content. She added monthly Q&A sessions, released updated modules as the design trends changed, and created an exclusive alumni group where students could network and share their progress. Her students didn't just finish the course—they became loyal advocates, referring new students and returning for advanced modules. Year after year, Karen's course continued to sell out, thanks to her commitment to providing ongoing value and optimizing the course experience.

Why Continuous Support and Optimization Matter

Karen's story highlights a vital lesson for course creators: **high-perceived value courses evolve**. Just because a course is successful at launch doesn't mean the work is done. To maintain relevance, engagement, and perceived value, you need to support your learners even after they've completed the course and consistently look for ways to improve the experience. Ongoing support and course optimization keep your course fresh, engaging, and tailored to your students' needs. This chapter will explore strategies for offering continuous support and how to use feedback to enhance future versions of your course.

Offering Ongoing Support: Keeping Learners Engaged Beyond the Course

One of the biggest mistakes course creators make is thinking their job ends when the final module is complete. But students often need support after the course ends—whether it's applying what they've learned or staying motivated to keep improving. Offering ongoing support helps maintain a relationship with your students and reinforces the value of your course.

Here's how you can offer meaningful ongoing support:

1. **Mentorship and Coaching** Offering ongoing mentorship or coaching after the course concludes can be an incredibly valuable way to support your learners. Whether it's through one-on-one sessions, group coaching, or office hours, continued access to you as the course creator gives students the chance to ask follow-up questions, clarify concepts, and get personalized feedback as they apply what they've learned.

Pro Tip: Create a mentorship package that students can opt into after completing the course, providing them with an extended learning experience.

2. **Live Q&A Sessions** Regular live Q&A sessions are a great way to keep students engaged after the course ends. These sessions allow students to ask questions, seek advice, and discuss their progress. Whether held monthly or quarterly, Q&A sessions give students direct access to you and an opportunity to connect with other learners.

Pro Tip: Record Q&A sessions and offer them as a resource for future students. This creates an ongoing library of answers and insights that adds long-term value to your course.

3. **Content Updates** Industries change, trends evolve, and new information becomes available. To keep your course relevant, offer periodic updates to your content. This could be as simple as updating statistics or adding new case studies, or as involved as creating new modules based on the latest developments in your field.

Pro Tip: Notify your students whenever new content is added. This encourages them to revisit the course and reinforces the perception that they're receiving continuous value.

4. **Certificates and Bonus Modules** Offering certificates of completion or bonus modules can keep students motivated and engaged. Certificates provide a tangible achievement that students can

share with their networks, while bonus modules or exclusive content give them a reason to stay involved after finishing the core course.

Pro Tip: Create an advanced module or bonus lesson for students who complete the course, offering deeper insights or advanced techniques that build on the core material.

Using Feedback and Data to Improve Future Versions of Your Course

One of the most powerful ways to optimize your course is through the feedback and data you collect from your students. Each cohort provides valuable insights into what's working and what could be improved. By consistently using this feedback, you can refine your course and create an even better experience for future students.

1. **Collecting Feedback** At the end of each course, send out a survey asking for student feedback. This could include questions about the course structure, content quality, instructor engagement, and any challenges they encountered. The more specific your questions, the more actionable insights you'll gain.

Pro Tip: Include open-ended questions like, "What was the most valuable part of the course?" and "What would you change or improve?" This will give students the chance to provide detailed feedback.

2. **Analyzing Data** Use the data available on your course platform to understand how students are engaging with the material. Look at metrics like completion rates, quiz scores, and time spent on each module. If you notice that students are

consistently dropping off at a particular point in the course, this could signal that the content needs to be adjusted.

Pro Tip: Compare data across multiple cohorts to identify trends. If multiple groups struggle with the same concept, it might be time to rework that section of the course.

3. **Making Improvements** Use the feedback and data you've gathered to continuously optimize your course. This could involve updating content, adding new resources, simplifying difficult concepts, or reorganizing the flow of the course. The goal is to keep refining the course so that each new cohort has a better experience than the last.

Pro Tip: Make improvements based on the most common feedback first. You don't need to overhaul your course after every cohort, but consistently implementing small changes will keep your course fresh and relevant.

Creating Alumni Groups and Offering Long-Term Engagement

One of the most effective ways to keep students engaged long after the course ends is by creating an alumni group. Alumni groups foster ongoing relationships, networking opportunities, and peer support—all of which increase the perceived value of your course and build loyalty to your brand.

1. **Alumni Networks** By creating a dedicated alumni group, either on a platform like Facebook or within your course community, you give students a place to continue learning and networking after the course

ends. Alumni networks provide a valuable space for students to share successes, ask for advice, and collaborate on future projects.

Pro Tip: Host exclusive events or webinars for your alumni group. This adds additional value and keeps your alumni engaged in your ecosystem.

2. **Offering Advanced Courses** After your students complete the initial course, many will be eager to continue their learning journey. Offering advanced courses or workshops tailored to your alumni group gives them the opportunity to dive deeper into the subject matter and continue working with you.

Pro Tip: Bundle advanced courses with alumni group access for a seamless transition from beginner to advanced learning.

Key Takeaways

Ongoing support and course optimization are essential for keeping your course relevant, valuable, and engaging over the long term. Here's how to support your students and improve your course:

1. **Offer Continuous Support**: Provide ongoing mentorship, live Q&A sessions, and updated content to keep students engaged long after the course ends.

2. **Use Feedback and Data**: Regularly collect feedback from students and analyze course engagement data to identify areas for improvement.

3. **Create Alumni Groups and Long-Term Engagement**: Build an alumni community where students can network and continue learning, and offer advanced courses to extend their learning journey.

By focusing on ongoing support and optimizing your course over time, you'll create a high-perceived value learning experience that keeps students coming back for more and sharing their positive experiences with others. In the next chapter, we'll explore how to scale your course business and create a sustainable, revenue-generating system.

CHAPTER 10:
Scaling Your Course Business

When Melanie launched her first course on wellness coaching, she never imagined it would lead to the thriving business she runs today. Initially, it was just a single course designed to help busy professionals manage stress and live healthier lives. The course did well, but Melanie wanted to make a bigger impact. So, she started thinking bigger—she bundled the course with new offerings, created advanced masterclasses, and began collaborating with other experts in the wellness space. Before long, Melanie's course was no longer a standalone product but the foundation of an entire suite of programs that generated consistent revenue and attracted a global audience. What started as a one-time launch evolved into a scalable, sustainable business that continues to grow year after year.

From Single Course to Course Empire: The Power of Scaling

Melanie's story highlights a powerful truth for course creators: once you've built a successful course, you have the potential to scale it into a full-fledged business. Scaling isn't just about making more money—it's about expanding your impact, reaching more people, and building a long-term legacy. What begins as a one-time course can evolve into a comprehensive learning ecosystem that generates ongoing revenue, even while you sleep.

Scaling your course business requires intentional strategies, systems, and partnerships. In this chapter, we'll explore how to turn your course into a sustainable, revenue-generating empire by leveraging automation, expanding your offerings, and collaborating with influencers and experts to expand your reach.

Leveraging Automation to Free Up Your Time

As your course grows, one of the first challenges you'll face is time management. Handling everything manually—enrollment, emails, course updates—will quickly become overwhelming. That's where automation comes in. By leveraging automation tools, you can streamline the administrative side of your business, freeing up your time to focus on higher-level tasks like creating new content or expanding your offerings.

1. **Automating Enrollment and Payments** One of the simplest ways to automate your course business is by setting up systems to handle enrollment and payments. Platforms like Teachable, Thinkific, and Kajabi allow you to automate the entire process—students can enroll, pay, and receive access to your course without you needing to lift a finger. This not only saves you time but also provides a seamless experience for your students.

Pro Tip: Set up automated payment plans for higher-ticket courses, making it easier for students to invest while ensuring consistent cash flow for your business.

2. **Automated Email Sequences** Automation isn't just for payments—it's also incredibly useful for staying connected with your students. By setting up automated email sequences, you can guide learners through your course, send reminders, and offer personalized support—all without having to manually send a single email. Tools like ConvertKit, ActiveCampaign, or Mailchimp can help you create these sequences.

Pro Tip: Create segmented email sequences for different stages of the student journey, such as onboarding, mid-course check-ins, and post-course follow-ups to keep students engaged.

3. **Course Updates and Feedback Loops** Automating feedback collection and course updates can help you keep your content fresh and relevant. Use automation tools to send out feedback surveys at key points in the course or after completion. This will help you gather insights that can guide future improvements.

Pro Tip: Incorporate feedback into an automated loop where students are prompted to review their progress, leave feedback, and receive updates on new content or features you've added to the course.

Expanding Your Offerings: Bundles, Masterclasses, and Certifications

Scaling your course business means thinking beyond a single course. Once your flagship course is established, there are several ways to expand your offerings and increase revenue by providing additional value to your students.

1. **Course Bundles** Bundling multiple courses together allows you to offer a more comprehensive learning experience while increasing the overall value for your students. For example, if you have a beginner course, consider creating intermediate and advanced courses that can be sold as a package. This not only boosts revenue but also encourages students to stay within your learning ecosystem longer.

Pro Tip: Offer exclusive pricing for students who purchase bundles, or add bonus content like worksheets or eBooks to make the bundle even more enticing.

2. **Masterclasses and Workshops** After students complete your initial course, they may be eager for more advanced, specialized training. Offering masterclasses or live workshops is a great way to cater to this demand while continuing to provide value. Masterclasses can be focused on niche topics or advanced techniques that go beyond the basics, positioning you as an expert in the field.

Pro Tip: Host live masterclasses periodically and record them for future use, allowing you to sell them as standalone products or part of a premium package.

3. **Certification Programs** If your course offers specialized training that students can use to enhance their careers, consider creating a certification program. Certification adds an extra layer of value to your course, as students can showcase their credentials to employers,

clients, or peers. Certifications also position your course as more authoritative, which can justify a higher price point.

Pro Tip: Offer tiered certifications based on different levels of expertise. For example, your base course might offer a "Certificate of Completion," while more advanced programs could offer "Professional Certification" for those who complete additional work or pass a final assessment.

Partnering with Influencers and Experts to Expand Your Reach

One of the fastest ways to scale your course business is by partnering with influencers or other experts in your industry. Strategic partnerships can help you reach new audiences, add credibility to your course, and expand your brand's visibility.

1. **Collaborate with Influencers** Influencers have the power to introduce your course to a larger, more diverse audience. By partnering with influencers who have a strong following in your niche, you can tap into their audience's trust and drive more enrollments. Collaborations can include joint webinars, guest appearances, or social media shoutouts.

Pro Tip: Look for influencers who align with your values and target audience. Authentic partnerships are more likely to succeed because the influencer's followers will sense that the collaboration is genuine.

2. **Bring in Guest Experts** Adding guest experts to your course can significantly boost its perceived value. Not only do guest experts provide additional insights and perspectives, but their involvement can also attract their

followers to your course. This strategy is especially effective for advanced courses or masterclasses where students expect in-depth, specialized knowledge.

Pro Tip: Structure your course so that each guest expert covers a unique topic that complements your core content. This keeps the course cohesive while expanding the range of expertise offered.

3. **Affiliate Programs** If you're looking to scale your course rapidly, consider creating an affiliate program where partners or past students earn a commission for promoting your course. Affiliates can act as ambassadors, sharing your course with their networks and driving new enrollments.

Pro Tip: Offer attractive commissions and provide your affiliates with high-quality marketing materials, such as graphics, sales copy, and social media posts, to make promoting your course easier and more effective.

Turning a One-Time Course Into an Evergreen Revenue Stream

One of the most powerful ways to scale your course business is by turning a live or cohort-based course into an **evergreen course**. Evergreen courses are pre-recorded and can be accessed by students at any time, which means you can continue to generate revenue without the need for constant live sessions or repeated launches.

1. **Repurposing Your Course** If you've already run a successful live course, you can easily repurpose the content into an evergreen format. This typically involves recording live sessions, editing them into polished

modules, and setting up an automated enrollment system. With the right setup, students can enroll and start learning at any time, making your course available on-demand.

Pro Tip: Combine your evergreen course with automated marketing funnels that include email sequences, retargeting ads, and upsell opportunities to maximize conversions.

2. **Create a Hybrid Model** Some students prefer the structure of live courses, while others like the flexibility of evergreen courses. You can create a hybrid model that offers both—students can access pre-recorded modules at their own pace but also join live Q&A sessions or coaching calls for added support. This gives you the best of both worlds, providing flexibility while maintaining a personal connection with your students.

Pro Tip: Use the hybrid model to offer personalized experiences at a premium price point, while still benefiting from the scalability of the evergreen format.

Key Takeaways

Scaling your course business is about more than just creating more content—it's about leveraging systems, expanding your offerings, and building partnerships that allow your business to grow sustainably. Here's how to turn your course into a scalable, revenue-generating empire:

1. **Leverage Automation**: Use tools to automate enrollment, payments, and email sequences, freeing up your time to focus on high-level business growth.

2. **Expand Your Offerings**: Create course bundles, masterclasses, and certification programs to provide ongoing value and increase revenue.

3. **Partner with Influencers and Experts**: Collaborate with influencers and guest experts to expand your reach and attract new students.

4. **Create Evergreen Courses**: Turn your live courses into evergreen products that generate revenue year-round without requiring constant launches or live sessions.

By implementing these strategies, you can transform a one-time course into a full-scale business that grows with you, creating a lasting legacy and a sustainable source of income. Now that you've learned how to scale your course business, it's time to take action and start building your own course empire.

CONCLUSION:
Your Gold Standard for Course Creation

As you've journeyed through this book, you've uncovered the key strategies to create high-perceived value courses that captivate your audience, inspire engagement, and drive sales. From laying the foundation with compelling course goals to building interactive learning experiences, designing visually stunning courses, and scaling your business for long-term success, you now have a comprehensive roadmap to transform your expertise into a thriving course empire.

The transformation you're about to create for your students is what sets your course apart. You're not just selling information—you're delivering a transformative experience that brings real results to your learners. Your course isn't just a product; it's a platform for empowerment, a space where your students will grow, learn, and reach their full potential.

You've learned how to:

- **Craft High-Value Courses**: By focusing on engagement, storytelling, and interactive learning, you've built courses that go beyond content delivery—they create memorable, life-changing experiences for your students.

- **Position and Market Your Course**: You've discovered how to position your course as the must-have solution, how to craft irresistible course descriptions that highlight transformation, and how to use pricing to communicate value.

- **Create Ongoing Engagement and Support**: By fostering a supportive learning community and offering continuous mentorship, live sessions, and content updates, you keep learners motivated long after the course ends.

- **Scale Your Business**: From bundling courses to creating evergreen products, you now know how to grow your course business into a sustainable, scalable venture that reaches new heights of success.

Your Time to Shine: Step Into Your Power as a Course Creator

You've got the blueprint. Now it's time to step into your power and put everything you've learned into action. You're more than capable of creating a course that stands out in the crowded online marketplace. The strategies you've learned are your toolkit to build a course that not only sells but also leaves a lasting impact on the lives of your students.

Remember, the journey of a course creator is not just about launching a single product—it's about building a legacy. By creating high-value, engaging courses, you're empowering others, growing your business, and stepping into your role as an expert and leader in your field.

So, what's next? It's time to take the leap. Embrace the journey of course creation, trust in the strategies you've learned, and build something truly remarkable. The world is waiting for what only you can offer.

Your gold standard of course creation starts now!

BOOKS IN THIS SERIES:
The Course Creator's Toolkit

The Course Creator's Toolkit series is designed for course creators who want to craft engaging, high-value courses that stand out in the crowded online education market. Based on real-world challenges faced by my clients, these books offer practical, step-by-step solutions to common pitfalls like low engagement, weak course design, or unclear outcomes.

Each chapter in the series feels like a personal coaching session with me, Meek Dual. I am passionate about helping others package their expertise into courses that not only sell but transform lives. You'll learn how to create interactive learning experiences, market your courses effectively, and build communities that keep learners engaged.

If you're ready to avoid the mistakes that hold most course creators back and build a profitable, high-perceived value course, this series is your blueprint for success.

Book 1: The Authority Advantage: Build Your Influence, Impact, and Income by Sharing What You Know

Are you ready to transform your expertise into influence, impact, and income?

In The Authority Advantage, entrepreneur and success coach Meek Dual reveals the proven strategies to help you become the go-to expert in your field. Whether you're an entrepreneur, coach, consultant, or creative professional, this book is your step-by-step guide to building lasting authority by leveraging the skills and knowledge you already possess.

Drawing from her own experiences and the journeys of countless successful clients, Meek shows you exactly how to:

- Find Your Zone of Genius: Identify the unique strengths that set you apart from the competition.

- Build a Personal Brand: Craft a brand that resonates with your ideal audience and communicates your value.

- Package Your Expertise: Turn your knowledge into profitable products and services, from online courses to consulting packages.

- Expand Your Influence: Use content creation and public speaking to grow your authority and reach more people.

- Stay Relevant: Learn how to continuously evolve as an expert and adapt to industry trends.

This book is packed with practical exercises, real-life case studies, and actionable steps that will help you create a legacy of influence while generating new income streams. You don't have to be a celebrity or a seasoned speaker to build authority. With the right mindset, tools, and persistence, anyone can become the expert others turn to for guidance and solutions.

Ready to amplify your authority and take your business to the next level?

Whether you're just starting out or you're ready to scale your impact, The Authority Advantage will give you the roadmap to success.

Get your copy today and start building the influence, impact, and income you deserve!

Book 2: Course Creator's Gold: Build Interactive Courses that Stick and SELL

Are you ready to transform your expertise into an engaging, high-value online course that captivates learners and generates revenue?

Course Creator's Gold is your step-by-step guide to creating courses that not only teach but inspire real transformation.

Packed with practical strategies and insights from my years of experience helping clients overcome the common pitfalls of course creation, this book is like having a personal coaching session with me, Meek Dual. I've helped countless women course creators who struggled with flat, disengaging content, unclear goals, and low sales. Now, I'm sharing the proven techniques that can help you avoid these challenges and build a course that not only sells but creates lasting impact.

Inside Course Creator's Gold, you'll learn:

- How to design interactive and dynamic learning experiences that keep your students engaged.

- Proven methods for crafting clear, actionable course goals that motivate learners.

- Practical tips for marketing your course and positioning it as a must-have solution in a crowded market.

- Strategies for building a supportive community around your course that fosters long-term engagement.

Whether you're just getting started or looking to refine your current course, Course Creator's Gold gives you the tools to create an online course that sells and delights learners. Start your journey toward course creation success today!

Book 3: Followers to Friends: Build Authentic Connections and Lasting Success Online

Ready to turn your followers into loyal, engaged supporters who trust and champion your brand?

In From Followers to Friends, success coach and creative visionary Meek Dual reveals the step-by-step strategies you need to build real, lasting connections online. Whether you're an entrepreneur, content creator, or professional seeking to grow your influence, this book is your roadmap to transforming followers into a true community—one rooted in trust and authenticity.

It's not about vanity metrics—it's about building trust. Through practical insights, real-life stories, and actionable steps, Meek shows you exactly how to:

- Build Trust: Learn why trust is the foundation of all online success and how to earn it through authenticity and consistency.

- Share Your Story: Craft an authentic digital persona that resonates deeply with your audience.

- Create Lasting Engagement: Develop strategies that encourage meaningful interactions and keep your audience coming back for more.

- Grow a Loyal Community: Move beyond just gaining followers and focus on building a supportive, engaged group of true fans.

- Handle Criticism with Grace: Turn negative feedback into opportunities for deeper connection and credibility.

With Meek's expert guidance, you'll learn how to build a sustainable online presence that doesn't just attract followers—it turns them into friends, loyal customers, and advocates for your brand. Packed with practical exercises and actionable advice, this book provides the tools you need to create real, lasting impact in the digital world.

Plus, as a bonus, you can access the FREE companion workbook to help you put these strategies into action and track your progress over the next 90 days.

Are you ready to transform your online presence and build a community that lasts?

Get your copy of From Followers to Friends today and start building the authentic connections that lead to lasting success!

ABOUT THE AUTHOR

Meek Dual is a learning experience designer, success coach, and creative visionary with a passion for helping women transform their expertise into high-impact, profitable online courses. As the founder of **MeekDual.com**, she has spent years empowering entrepreneurs, professionals, and creators to build engaging learning experiences that not only educate but inspire real change.

With a unique blend of storytelling, strategic design, and educational expertise, Meek has built a thriving business that serves clients worldwide. Her innovative approach—known as "Meek's Magic"—combines practical strategies with creative insights to help her clients bring their visions to life.

As a single mother of children with learning challenges, Meek understands the power of perseverance, faith, and the ability to turn challenges into strengths. Her journey has shaped her into the mentor and guide she is today, and she is deeply committed to helping others succeed without sacrificing well-being or personal growth.

In **"Course Creator's Gold,"** Meek shares her proven strategies for building high-value, engaging courses that stick and sell, empowering women to step into their roles as experts and create a lasting legacy through education.

You can connect with Meek and learn more about her work at **MeekDual.com**.

COURSE CREATOR'S GOLD

www.ingramcontent.com/pod-product-compliance
Lightning Source LLC
Chambersburg PA
CBHW050317230526
45471CB00005B/2224